IRAQ:
STRATEGIC RECONCILIATION, TARGETING, AND KEY LEADER ENGAGEMENT

Jeanne F. Hull

September 2009

ISBN 1-58487-405-8

FOREWORD

Military commanders and diplomats in Iraq and Afghanistan have been meeting with important local officials since the inception of those conflicts. These Key Leader Engagements (or KLE as they are now termed) have aided commanders and diplomats alike in furthering their objectives by establishing productive relationships with those who know and understand Iraq's complex human terrain best—the Iraqis. However, these engagements frequently take place on ad-hoc bases and are rarely incorporated into other counterinsurgency operations and strategies. In some cases, unit commanders fail to see the utility of using KLE at all—an oversight that contributes to deteriorating security situations and loss of popular support.

This Letort Paper discusses KLE as a nonlethal option for countering insurgent organizations. As was the case with the Anbar Awakening, outreach to insurgent organizations through KLE can be both an economy of force measure and, in some circumstances, could be more effective than engaging insurgent organizations with lethal force. The challenge with insurgent outreach to KLE, though, is that it must be tied to a legitimate host-nation government effort towards reconciliation or, at a minimum, accommodation with the insurgent organizations in question.

Through the lens of the Multi-National Forces-Iraq Force Strategic Engagement Cell (FSEC), the author also illustrates how KLEs can be incorporated as targets in the U.S. military's targeting process. FSEC's mission to reach out to Iraq-based insurgent organizations who sought reconciliation with the Iraqi government was entirely based in KLE-related targeting. FSECs activities, therefore, present a suitable case to study how including KLE as "targets" within the targeting process can maximize the utility of the relationships commanders and diplomats alike establish during counterinsurgency and nation-building operations. The operations of this strategic engagement cell also demonstrate the employment of KLE as a part of Information Operations, and the challenges associated with developing and refining intelligence to support KLE targeting. The other challenges FSEC personnel dealt with highlight some additional difficulties commanders and diplomats face with respect to KLE operations with emphasis on managing expectations, continuity, capability, and synchronization of effort. Finally, FSEC's endeavors in Iraq underscore the utility of outreach to both local leaders and insurgent populations in counterinsurgency operations.

DOUGLAS C. LOVELACE, JR.
Director
Strategic Studies Institute

ABOUT THE AUTHOR

JEANNE F. HULL, a captain in the U.S. Army, is a Military Intelligence Officer at the Training and Doctrine Command, Washington, DC; and Ph.D. Candidate at Princeton University, New Jersey. She received her commission from West Point in 2000, and her first duty assignment was as a Company Executive Officer in Ft. Lewis, Washington. After September 11, 2001, she spent 10 months in Sarajevo, Bosnia, as a counterterrorism analyst on the Stabilization Force, Joint and Inter-Agency Task Force (JIATF). Captain Hull later served in Iraq as the Division Targeting Intelligence Officer for the 101st Airborne Division during the Iraq invasion and post-conflict support and stability operations from 2003-04. She returned to Iraq 3 months after redeployment to work as a special assistant to the Commanding General for the newly formed Multi-National Security Transition Command-Iraq (MNSTC-I), then Lieutenant General David Petraeus. In late 2007, Captain Hull went back to Iraq and worked as an adviser to the Iraqi Directorate General of Intelligence and Security (DGIS) before transferring to the MNF-I Force Strategic Engagement Cell (FSEC) as a strategic engager. She will join the West Point Department of Social Sciences as a professor of International Relations in the summer of 2009. Captain Hull holds a Masters in Public Affairs from the Woodrow Wilson School for Public and International Affairs through the Army's Advanced Civil Schooling (ACS) program, Princeton University, New Jersey. She is currently attending the Military Intelligence Captain's Career Course (MICCC).

SUMMARY

When discussing new approaches to the insurgency in Afghanistan, General David Petraeus emphasized that his experiences in Iraq had reinforced the notion that "You cannot kill or capture your way out of an insurgency." That statement acknowledges that success for U.S. forces in counterinsurgency operations is the result of a combination of persuasive and coercive measures applied against insurgent organizations and their bases of support. Some of the key principles behind that statement also suggest that the "bad guys" can possibly be or become the "good guys," in that some insurgent leaders and groups can transition from violence and dissention to constructive activities. That transition requires that the insurgents be encouraged to reconcile their differences with the establishments they are resisting. Setting the conditions for those transitions at all levels of a conflict requires skillful, nuanced negotiations between leaders or representatives of insurgent groups, legitimate government forces, and representatives of a neutral or intervening force as appropriate.

Coalition military outreach to Sunni shaykhs working with al-Qaida in Anbar province revealed how Key Leader Engagement (KLE) with members of the insurgent population could be a useful, if not necessary, tool for commanders in Iraq. Multi-National Force-Iraq (MNF-I) Commander General Petraeus subsequently supported the establishment of a cell specifically designed to conduct KLE with other Iraqi insurgent organizations at the strategic level. The mission of that strategic-level KLE cell, the Force Strategic Engagement Cell (FSEC), required it to conduct KLE with members of Sunni and Shi'a resistance elements and leaders to bring them into a political accommodation with the Iraqi government—a first step towards reconciliation.

FSEC's establishment and subsequent operations did not want for challenges or detractors. To begin with, many seasoned commanders and diplomats viewed outreach to insurgent organizations as a dangerous and untested new enterprise. In reality, that type of outreach had been used in previous insurgencies and other conflicts effectively, to include Vietnam. In addition, although U.S. military training centers had begun to introduce the topic of negotiation in preparation for combat deployments in Iraq and Afghanistan, no template or structure existed for incorporating the routine or special engagements that military leaders conducted with members of the host nation who had the ability to impact their area of responsibility into other operations. By the same token, most of the Coalition personnel assigned to FSEC had little or no preparation for conducting strategic engagements and/or brokering dialogue between Iraqi insurgents and the Iraqi government. In response to these challenges and others, the FSEC leadership applied some precedents from other theaters and both principles and doctrine of counterinsurgency and conflict resolution that appeared to suit the mission requirements to construct processes and mechanisms to assist them in achieving their objectives.

This Letort Paper uses FSEC's operations in Iraq from 2008-09 to illustrate how KLE can be incorporated into existing targeting, information operations, and intelligence doctrine for counterinsurgency operations. It opens with a description of the principles of counterinsurgency and conflict resolution that form the basis for effective insurgent outreach and thus FSEC operations. It further highlights how FSEC's employment of the U.S. military's targeting process and how other U.S. agencies—including the U.S. Department of State—involved in counterinsurgency operations might incorporate those processes into their own engagements abroad. The paper then identifies some of the challenges and risks associated with FSEC's mission and recommends how insurgent outreach and other KLE operations might better be incorporated with concurrent operations in counterinsurgency.

IRAQ:
STRATEGIC RECONCILIATION, TARGETING, AND KEY LEADER ENGAGEMENT

The supreme excellence is not to win a hundred victories in a hundred battles. The supreme excellence is to subdue the armies of your enemies without even having to fight them.

Sun Tzu

They will conquer, but they will not convince.

Miguel de Unamuno

INTRODUCTION

When discussing new approaches to the insurgency in Afghanistan, General David Petraeus emphasized that his experiences in Iraq had reinforced the notion that "You cannot kill or capture your way out of an insurgency."[1] That statement acknowledges that success for U.S. forces in counterinsurgency (COIN) operations is the result of a combination of persuasive and coercive measures applied against insurgent organizations and their bases of support. Some of the key principles behind that statement also suggest that the "bad guys" can possibly be or become the "good guys" in that some insurgent leaders and groups can transition from violence and dissention to constructive activities. That transition requires that the insurgents be encouraged to reconcile their differences with the establishments they are resisting. Setting the conditions for those transitions at all levels of a conflict requires skillful, nuanced negotiations between leaders or representatives of insurgent groups, legitimate

1

government forces, and representatives of a neutral or intervening force, as appropriate.

Some Coalition commanders in Iraq recognized the importance of developing rapport and relationships with local leaders and influential people early in post-invasion Iraq. Others did not see the utility of that dialogue, and dissent and violence increased in those areas.[2] Discussions with leaders of insurgent organizations did not surface until sometime later, largely in response to constraints imposed on Coalition civilian and diplomatic personnel not to engage with "terrorists" and the novelty of the concepts to commanders who spent most of their time fighting insurgents. Beginning in 2004 and 2005, however, U.S. military personnel initiated dialogue with members of Iraqi Sunni tribes in Anbar and Baghdad provinces who had begun to tire of their alliances with al-Qaida in Iraq. Although controversial, the outreach substantially reduced violence in those provinces—at least in the short term.[3]

That outreach in Anbar revealed how Key Leader Engagement (KLE) with members of the insurgent population could be a useful—if not necessary—tool for commanders in Iraq. Multi-National Force-Iraq (MNF-I) Commander General Petraeus subsequently supported the establishment of a cell specifically designed to conduct KLE with other Iraqi insurgent organizations at the strategic level. The mission of that strategic-level KLE cell, the Force Strategic Engagement Cell (FSEC), required it to conduct KLE with members of Sunni and Shi'a resistance elements and leaders to bring them into a political accommodation with the Iraqi government—a first step towards reconciliation.[4]

FSEC's establishment and subsequent operations did not want for challenges or detractors. To begin with, many seasoned commanders and diplomats viewed outreach to insurgent organizations as a dangerous and untested new enterprise. In reality, that type of outreach had been used in previous insurgencies and other conflicts effectively, to include Vietnam. In addition, although U.S. military training centers had begun to introduce the topic of negotiation in preparation for combat deployments in Iraq and Afghanistan,[5] no template or structure existed for incorporating the routine or special engagements that military leaders conducted with members of the host-nation who had the ability to impact their area of responsibility into other operations. By the same token, most of the Coalition personnel assigned to FSEC had little or no preparation for conducting strategic engagements and/or brokering dialogue between Iraqi insurgents and the Iraqi government. In response to these challenges and others, the FSEC leadership applied some precedents from other theaters and both principles and doctrine of COIN and conflict resolution that appeared to suit the mission requirements to construct processes and mechanisms to assist them in achieving their objectives.

Despite the fact that FSEC operations were based on both precedents from previous conflicts and hallmark COIN tenets, the conduct of these operations was criticized by a number of parties, including units whose focus was defeating insurgent organizations via coercive measures, and career diplomats from the U.S. mission in Iraq. Those that sought to defeat Iraq's multi-faceted insurgency with force were dismissive of the value of dialogue, and argued that hostile elements would use that dialogue to cover planning and organizing for future operations. Interestingly, diplomats and others working to defeat the insurgency by persuasive means were also critical. Describing FSEC as a "capability without a mission," some U.S.

Foreign Service officers acknowledged the utility of using military processes and techniques to organize what was essentially a diplomatic mission, but assessed that trained, experienced diplomats were better suited to conduct the requisite dialogue.

The purpose of this paper is to use FSEC's operations in Iraq from 2008-09 to illustrate how KLE can be incorporated into existing targeting, information operations, and intelligence doctrine for COIN operations. It opens with a description of the principles of COIN and conflict resolution that form the basis for effective insurgent outreach and thus FSEC operations. It continues with a detailed description of FSEC's organization, structure, and conduct of operations, followed by the doctrinal basis for FSEC's procedures for targeting, information operations, and intelligence as outlined by the U.S. Army and Marine Corps Counterinsurgency manual, Field Manual (FM) 3-24.[6] It further highlights how FSEC's employment of the U.S. military's targeting process and how other U.S. agencies—including the U.S. Department of State—involved in COIN operations might incorporate those processes into their own engagements abroad. The paper concludes by identifying some of the challenges and risks associated with FSEC's mission, and by recommending how insurgent outreach and other KLE operations might better be incorporated with concurrent operations in COIN.

Importantly, this paper does not attempt to suggest that KLE is a new concept or technique as KLE has been ongoing in the Iraq and Afghanistan conflicts for years. The paper also does not aim to show that strategic KLE or FSEC was the most important factor in achieving stability in Iraq. Rather, the paper's objectives are to demonstrate how incorporating KLE into the targeting process—and conducting targeted engagements with insurgents and other hostile elements in particular—can be a valuable tool for military, diplomatic, and other intervening forces in COIN operations.

CONTROL IN COIN AND CONFLICT RESOLUTION

Although FSEC operations (and KLE with insurgents in particular) were viewed as somewhat radical by Iraq-based coalition military commanders and diplomats, the key concepts behind these operations were not new. FSEC operations were based on both precedents from similar environments as well as some of the basic precepts of COIN and conflict resolution identified by theorists and practitioners alike. Specifically, counterinsurgents who intervene in a conflict face a number of challenges when they work with a legitimate host-nation government to quell an insurgency. They lack an understanding of the physical terrain as well as the human terrain in an area—the cultural and social norms that guide behavior and choices within a population. The host-nation government they are working with may or may not be viewed as legitimate and, in those areas under insurgent control, the insurgent groups have legitimacy. Rather than expend considerable resources attempting to take over insurgent strongholds and controlled areas by force, it would be more efficient for counterinsurgents to find means by which the host-nation and insurgent organizations can find common ground and, ultimately, reconcile with each other. The conflict then, in theory, could transition from one involving military force to more of a political battle, thereby allowing counterinsurgents to step back.

Theory and Practice: Intervention, "Hearts and Minds," and Regaining Control.

Conflicts involving insurgencies are typically messy affairs that tend to be both violent and prolonged. Indeed, the very nature of insurgencies—that forces opposed to a legitimate government and its military must maximize the use of nontraditional "intangibles" such as propaganda and time and unconventional tactics and techniques to wear down the initially stronger and more power government forces—is what makes them so.[7] Sometimes the conflicts become so violent and destabilizing that outside actors attempt to intervene in the conflict to end the violence, protect their interests abroad, etc. States and forces that intervene or otherwise become involved in these types of conflicts often find themselves confronted with highly complex and diverse situations in which they and their forces are viewed as outsiders, irrespective of whether or not their intentions are good. The "outsider" status also entails its own set of challenges including understanding (or misunderstanding) the physical terrain, the underlying roots of the conflict, and the culture and society of the areas in which they operate—factors that only become more important as the conflict continues.

FM 3-24 notes that insurgents and counterinsurgents are competing for the same key terrain in those conflicts—the popular support of the people stuck in the middle. The manual also notes that "insurgents use numerous methods to generate popular support," including persuasive and coercive techniques.[8] Insurgents have some distinct advantages over intervening counterinsurgents when it comes to competing for popular support. In particular, insurgents are present among the population and fundamentally understand the society in which they operate. Those fighting the insurgents—particularly those not native to an area—generally have more limited means at their disposal. Even if the intervening forces are ostensibly present to provide tangible benefits to a population—enforcing and monitoring peace, provision of humanitarian aide, etc.—their status as outsiders combined with an indeterminate length of stay frequently renders their motivations and activities highly suspect and vulnerable to insurgent propaganda campaigns.

Counterinsurgents of the 20th century repeatedly asserted that "winning the hearts and minds of the civilian population is one of the key elements of winning a war."[9] Despite the broad and often inaccurate context in which this expression is used today, a successful "hearts and minds strategy" in its original form is one that isolates insurgents physically and psychologically from a population,[10] which is much more difficult in practice than it sounds. We have already addressed some of the challenges intervening forces face when attempting to isolate the population from insurgents. These difficulties tend to increase when a population is under the complete control of an insurgent organization. An insurgent-controlled population may not wish to transition back to government control because the insurgent organization provides all the basic needs—security and basic services—that a government cannot or will not provide. In a detailed study of the Greek Civil War (1946-49), Stathis Kalyvas found that regardless of whether an insurgent group or the government controlled an area, there was relatively little violence or instability in areas where there was complete control.[11] The lack of resistance in those areas suggested that such control was acceptable to the people living there, and that at least basic needs were being met. David Elliot found similar outcomes in his study of the Mekong Delta during the Vietnam conflict. In that case, the Viet Cong lost control in areas of the Mekong Delta because they could not provide security for the peasants, and Viet Cong policies prevented many of the peasants in that area from access to their source of livelihood. The peasants responded by cooperating with U.S. and other forces working with the South Vietnamese government to rid the area of the Viet Cong.[12] A more recent example of how insurgent control might be acceptable to a population is Hizballah's activities in areas of southern Lebanon and Beirut. In select areas, Hizballah is viewed more positively than the government since it provides both security and essential services to the population through social and charitable organizations.[13] If the population is satisfied with the group in control of an area, it will be difficult for counterinsurgents to convince the population that the insurgent activity there is undesirable, much less wrest control from the insurgent.

Transitioning Insurgent Groups, Dialogue, and Veto Players.

One means of ending a conflict involving an insurgency is by encouraging insurgent organizations to stop fighting and enter the political process.[14] Examples of insurgent groups that transitioned to the political process (with varying degrees of success) include Hamas and al-Fatah in Palestine, armed groups during the Bosnia conflict, and Sinn Fein in Northern Ireland. In those cases, the insurgent groups saw an opportunity to achieve some of their aims more effectively via political participation than violence.

They were also able to organize political parties that were recognized—however grudgingly in some cases—by the governments they fought against.[15]

Transitioning an insurgent group into a recognized, legitimate political entity is not a speedy or simple process. It requires—among other things—an insurgent leadership prepared to risk losing its *raison d'etat,* identity, and prestige, and a *legitimate* government leadership equally as willing to risk political capital by conceding to the demands of a group that attempted to achieve its aims by force. Host-nation government legitimacy—defined here as the degree to which an organization or entity is thought worthy of support— is essential to success.[16] In his study of Hizballah in Lebanon, Cliff Staten argues that, for Hizballah to make a successful transition, both Hizballah and the Lebanese government must acknowledge that the benefits of Hizballah's participation in the political process outweigh the costs and risks associated with that transition.[17] If an insurgent organization and the people who accept its system of governance in insurg-ent-controlled areas do not believe the government is capable of meeting their physical and political needs, they will not see any benefit to rejoining the political process. Under these circumstances, both parties must recognize the legitimacy of the other.

The presence of an intervening force or party can sometimes assist with the process by attempting to establish or reestablish a relationship between a legitimate government and insurgent. Dialogue is one means of opening communications channels, encouraging accommodation and, ultimately, reconciliation between government and insurgent. Traditionally, a state's diplomatic corps is responsible for resolving interstate conflict through dialogue. Some nations, including the United States and United

Kingdom (UK) also on occasion, use their diplomatic representatives to adjudicate intrastate conflicts in the Middle East and Europe via dialogue, their involvement in the Arab-Israeli and Bosnian conflicts being examples of the practice. Less common, however, are circumstances in which states use their diplomatic corps or designated policy officials to resolve an intrastate conflict in which that state's own military and civilians are targeted by insurgents (in addition to the local government's forces). In fact, insurgents attacking an intervening state's forces and the civilians they protect are sometimes labeled as "terrorists" or "hostile militias" and tend to be precluded from dialogue with a state's official diplomats or other policy representatives. In those cases, the diplomatic corps or mission within a country must use the resources it has at hand while still fulfilling its policy requirements, including military forces operating in the country.

There are two keys to success for brokering reconciliation initiatives through dialogue. First, the intervening forces must engage with government and insurgent leaders best able to influence their followers to pursue dialogue over violence. A study on contemporary conflict resolution notes the importance of insurgent groups swaying popular support— "even then, their ability to carry skeptical factions and constituencies is essential for settlement."[18] Like political parties in democratic societies, insurgent groups contain select personnel who have the ability to sway opinions and, consequently, the majority of a group. Known as "veto players" in political science literature, these influential insurgent group members can make or break dialogue and efforts to broker reconciliation.[19] The government and intervening force are, therefore, better served by engaging in dialogue with those veto players and their representatives than ones who, while important, lack the clout and persuasiveness of others.

Second, the intervening force must be able to link any initiatives involving dialogue with an insurgent population with the host-nation government or its appointed representatives. Although the outreach between U.S. military forces and Anbari shayks in Iraq was initially successful in combating al-Qaida's support in Iraq, dissention surfaced when the Iraqi government refused to acknowledge or assume control for the initiative and its requirement to integrate members of Anbari tribes into the Iraqi Security Forces or other salaried positions. Because the Iraqi government had no buy-in to the original initiative, they were suspicious of the concept and were unhappy with Coalition implementation. They were also skeptical about the political party formed by the Anbari shaykhs involved in the initiative, and implemented legislation that could have prevented that party and its affiliates from participating in the political process. Although the Iraqi government eventually found an Iraqi way to assume responsibility for the effort, the transition to Iraqi control was tenuous for months, and the initiative very nearly fell apart. The relations between the Iraqi government and the Sunni shaykhs who disavowed their allegiance to al-Qaida remains tenuous to this day.[20]

Summary of the Theory and Application in Iraq.

In a conflict involving an insurgency, governments and intervening forces are competing with an insurgent population for the hearts and minds of a population. In areas under insurgent control, insurgents are sometimes able to provide security and basic services for their people; activities that make the return to government control appear unnecessary and/or undesirable. Furthermore, retaking physical control of those areas by force is costly in terms of resources and human life. Therefore, it is in the interests of a government and an intervening force to transition the insurgent group to the political process and, in so doing, regain control of those territories controlled by the insurgent population. Such a transition is only possible, however, if the host-nation government is viewed as legitimate by the insurgent organization and the population under its control and if the intervening force links its reconciliation efforts with the government. An intervening force can, furthermore, help broker that transition only if the host-nation government is on-board with the proposed transition and initiatives that lead to that transition.

As 2005 came to a close, it was clear that Coalition forces were fighting a variety of insurgent groups in Iraq and watching the country descend into civil war. Not only were Sunni and Shi'a insurgent organizations attempting to expel the "occupation" forces from their homeland, but some had been inspired to kill their fellow Iraqis as well. This complex situation combining both an anti-occupation and anti-Iraqi government insurgency and civil war necessitated some drastic measures, including a significant force build-up to quell the short-term violence. Coalition leaders also recognized that stemming the tide of violence required both military force and diplomatic involvement. Some Coalition units, including those in Anbar, seized the initiative and conducted some KLE with insurgents to broker discussions in Anbar and some areas of Baghdad.[21] However, there was little to no Iraqi government involvement or buy-in initially and no Coalition organization authorized to engage the Iraqi insurgent leadership or at the strategic level. In July 2007, Coalition Forces commander General Petraeus ordered the establishment of the FSEC at the behest of his UK Deputy, Lieutenant General Graeme Lamb. Lieutenant General Lamb had some experience working with insurgent groups in Northern Ireland and thought a similar outreach program would be effective in Iraq.[22]

The purpose of FSEC at the time was to fill a diplomatic gap—to generate an organization within the Coalition willing and able to open communications channels via discreet dialogue with serving and former members of Iraq's insurgent organizations. FSEC's objective was—through that dialogue—to set the conditions for reconciliation between Sunni and Shi'a insurgent groups and the Iraqi government. General Petraeus further described the role of FSEC as to use KLE with those groups ". . . to understand various local situations and dynamics, and then—in full coordination with the Iraqi government—to engage tribal leaders, local government leaders, and, in some cases, insurgent and opposition elements . . ."[23]

At that time, Prime Minister Nuri al-Maliki had his own reconciliation cell entitled the "Iraq Follow-on Committee for National Reconciliation." FSEC liaison with the Iraqi reconciliation cell, coupled with simultaneous outreach to insurgent organizations, marked the initiation of a new chapter in Iraq COIN operations—the acknowledgement that, even if policy requirements forbade state diplomatic representatives from engaging with so-called "terrorist" organizations, a military strategic engagement cell could establish those relationships in the interests of national reconciliation and the greater Joint Campaign Plan objective of ensuring sustainable security and stability in Iraq. In offering elements of the insurgent groups an opportunity to reconcile to the Iraqi government (and, by default, the Coalition), General Petraeus and Lieutenant General Lamb hoped to isolate members of those organizations who would fight to the death from those that sought peaceful, constructive alternatives to fighting. The FSEC founders and leadership readily acknowledged that the Coalition could only do so much—at some stage in the process Iraqi government buy-in and ability to carry the dialogue forward would make or break any reconciliation initiatives.

The fundamental principle guiding FSEC operations was the idea that persuading select individuals from Iraqi insurgent groups (or those sympathetic to them) to engage in dialogue with the Iraqi government was more efficient than trying to destroy the groups with military force. Because the insurgents were already in control of large swaths of territory in some Iraqi provinces, Coalition forces and the Iraqi government could gain control of those places more efficiently by engaging with insurgent groups than battling for territory one kilometer or village at a time. By identifying and engaging the veto players—the key insurgent leaders and their supporters—within the insurgent organizations, the Coalition and Iraqi government could encourage them to address their concerns via the political process and let them figure out how best to direct the "hearts and minds" of their adherents to pursue the political alternative. Those who chose not to take the proffered olive branch would be exposed and identified as "irreconcilable" and would be subject to elimination by military force.

FSEC STRUCTURE, OPERATIONS, AND THE U.S MILITARY TARGETING PROCESS

The FSEC structure and conduct of operations evolved over time to meet the requirements of a dynamic insurgent situation in Iraq and the changing policies and approaches of the Iraqi government. The comparatively small cell of 30 or so Coalition military personnel organized itself based on the known structure of the Iraq-based insurgent groups and Iraqi government officials. That structure was modified based on what the FSEC Director assessed as being the main emphasis of Coalition Iraqi government reconciliation objectives. FSEC operations were grounded in the U.S. targeting process where the "targets" became personnel with whom the FSEC director wished to conduct KLE, and the "effects" were linked to the outcomes of those KLE processes. In essence, FSEC's coordinated efforts with other cells, directorates, and agencies operating in Iraq became a medium for KLE targeting synchronization. Specifics for how FSEC was structured and how it used the targeting process to direct its operations are outlined below.

FSEC Structure.

FSEC was a small cell of 30 personnel — primarily Coalition military officers — directed by a UK General Officer. All FSEC directors had previous experience in the conflict in Northern Ireland and in Iraq or Afghanistan. To link this largely Coalition military effort with civilian policymakers, U.S. Ambassador to Iraq Ryan Crocker appointed a senior U.S. State Department Foreign Service Officer (FSO) as his representative in the organization to work in concert

with the FSEC Director. The Director was assigned
a Chief of Staff at the rank of Colonel or equivalent
who was responsible for supervising the day-to-day
operations of the cell, synchronizing FSEC operations
with other directorates within the MNF-I staff,
and managing the administrative functions of the
organization. FSEC was also equipped with a small
intelligence cell with a reach-back capability into U.S.
and UK national intelligence agencies and the MNF-I
joint military and civilian intelligence cell, the C-2.

FSEC was organized along the assessed structure of
the Iraqi insurgency in 2007. The Directorate developed
"lanes" whose task was to identify and establish
relationships with members of the three main groups
that could work within the reconciliation process: (1) to
liaise with representatives and organizations working
reconciliation initiatives within the Iraqi Government,
(2) to conduct outreach to Sunni dissident and
insurgent organizations, and (3) to conduct outreach
to Shi'a dissident and insurgent organizations. Each
lane contained a primary "engager" responsible
for developing relationships with personnel in his
or her area of responsibility, a lane deputy, and an
intelligence analyst who specialized in either the Iraqi
Government, Sunni insurgent groups, and/or Shi'a
insurgent groups. A generalized structure for FSEC
with the proposed ranks/grades for each position is
shown in Table 1.

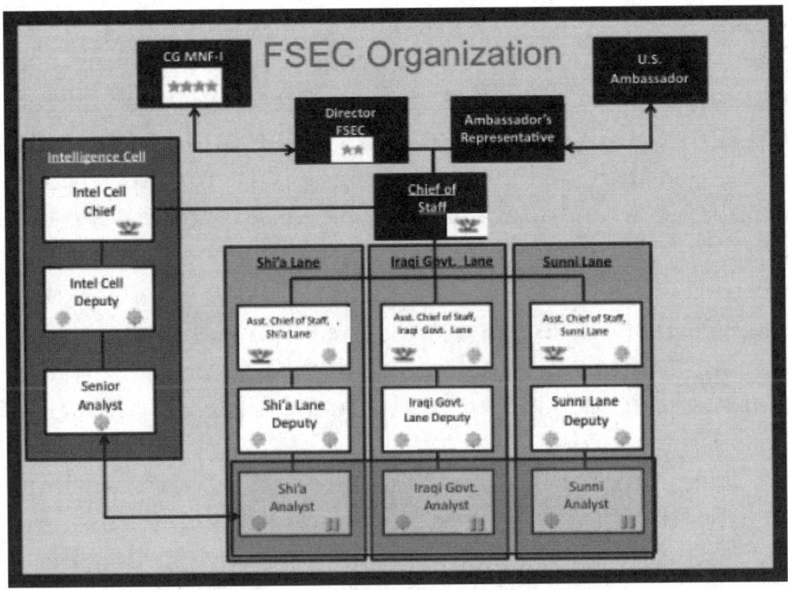

Table 1: Generalized Structure for FSEC with Recommended Ranks by Position.

Targeting in Counterinsurgency.

Much of the strategy for (and rationale behind) the KLE that the FSEC director chose to conduct was grounded in the U.S. military targeting process. As is the case with most nonlethal targeting missions, however, there were some important differences in execution of the targeting process between FSEC operations and traditional targeting in conventional military operations.

The traditional U.S. military targeting cycle is a continuous process involving four primary steps. The commanders first *decide* which targets to engage and then use available assets to *detect* the targets by identifying their location. Both of these steps are very much intelligence-driven. The commander then tasks his assets to *deliver* lethal or nonlethal measures to the target to achieve his desired effect for that target. In conventional warfare, the commander typically assigns a unit to destroy a target with military force. Finally, commanders designate assets to *assess* the effectiveness of that delivery and whether or not the desired effect was achieved. The cycle then begins anew. All of the effects are supposed to be synchronized during targeting synchronization meetings, and the commander provides his direction during routine targeting boards.

Targeting for unconventional and COIN operations follows the same process, but tends to have a different focus and the desired effects are more varied. Recalling that targeting in COIN operations should be effects-oriented, FM 3-24 reiterates that "commanders and staffs [should] use the targeting process to achieve the effects that support [Lines of Operation] in a COIN campaign plan."[24] FM 3-24 also reminds commanders that "it is important to understand that targeting is done for all operations, not just attacks against insurgents," and explains that in COIN

> . . . the focus for targeting is on people, both insurgents and non-combatants . . . effective targeting options, both lethal and non-lethal, to achieve the effects that support the commander's objectives . . . non-lethal targets are usually *more important than lethal targets in counterinsurgency;* they are never less important.[25]

The FM further identifies prospective nonlethal targets as "people like community leaders and those insurgents who should be engaged through outreach, negotiation, meetings, and other interaction."[26] The manual goes on to illustrate how commanders should use the targeting process to identify which "community leaders" and insurgents should be engaged and means of obtaining access to those individuals. If people are the primary targets in COIN and non-lethal targets tend to be more important, the desired effects and how to achieve them become significantly more varied and complex than in conventional military operations.

There is plenty of precedent for using the targeting process for nonlethal targets in conflicts from Vietnam to the present, including Iraq.[27] During stability operations in Mosul from 2003-04, the 101st Airborne Division (Air Assault) developed an Integrated Effects Working Group (IE-WG) as a targeting synchronization meeting for all operations in the 101st's Area of Responsibility (AOR), both lethal and nonlethal. The working group focused on a variety of nonlethal operations, including meetings and KLE with important Iraqi nationals and Ninawa provincial government officials to further ongoing reconstruction and stabilization activities.[28] However, the IEWG did not specifically address a strategy for engaging the local government and its opponents for reconciliation purposes—much of the required "reconciliation" in Ninawa province, including some contentions situations in Tall 'Afar and Zumar, was conducted on an ad-hoc basis as situations developed, rather than as part of a deliberate targeting process. Since then, various U.S. units in Iraq have applied similar targeting boards to integrate lethal and nonlethal effects, including KLE. For example, in 2008 the 4th Infantry Division conducted KLE associated with reconciliation initiatives between different groups in Baghdad through the activities of a small reconciliation cell and a cell operating out of the Division G-7 shop. The integration of KLE into the targeting process across theater has, however, not been uniformly applied.

FSEC Operations and the Targeting Process.

In accordance with FM 3-24's guidelines for conducting targeting operations in COIN, FSEC used the targeting process to achieve goals within the reconciliation line of operation as outlined in the MNF-I Joint Campaign Plan (JCP).[29] FSEC initial operations included establishing liaison with the Iraqi government reconciliation cell with officers from the FSEC Iraqi Government lane. Outreach to Sunni and Shi'a insurgent organizations proceeded through a planning process involving a weekly Engagement Synchronization Meeting (ESM) and Engagement Planning Meeting (EPM), which served as target synchronization meetings and targeting boards respectively. KLE "targets" for FSEC's unique mission included influential people within IFCNR or others within the Iraqi government, members of Sunni or Shi'a insurgent organizations who had either reached out to coalition forces or otherwise indicated a desire to participate in dialogue, and prospective interlocutors who could act on behalf of FSEC in bringing in key players from all elements in theater.

FSEC used the ESM to synchronize its KLE targets with engagements conducted by other directorates, U.S. and U.K diplomatic missions in the country, and other agencies who had equity in those targets. Representatives of these organizations were invited to attend the meeting and discuss their own engagements as FSEC personnel briefed their target list. The ESM also allowed FSEC to socialize some of its strategy and approach with different Iraqi insurgent groups with those other agencies and elicit feedback and requests for additional information.

During the EPMs (targeting board), the FSEC Director *decided* which proposed engagement targets were either (1) unsuitable for engagement, (2) required deconfliction with other agencies, and/or (3) would be more appropriate to engage at a more opportune time. Based on the priority of the targets to his mission requirements, the director then decided which assets to *deliver* to each proposed engagement target; he differentiated between the engagements he would conduct, those the Ambassador's representative would conduct, and those the lane leaders and cultural advisor would conduct. The director also identified the location and medium in which to conduct the KLE based on known or assessed meeting requirements. For example, FSEC might have damaged or degraded an engagement targets' reputations and, thus, their influence if the fact they were meeting with Coalition personnel became known.

Following receipt of the director's guidance, the lane leaders arranged for the *delivery* phase of the process; setting up meetings between FSEC personnel and the engagement targets. Once the meeting took place, a member of FSEC would write an executive summary of the engagement outlining the key talking points from both FSEC and the KLE target, requests, and a brief *assessment* of the effects of the meeting. The *assess* phase lasted long after the engagement, and subsequent engagements often resulted in reassessments of the value of the engagement target, whether or not the engagement was achieving the desired effects, and the identification of any other effects FSEC might be able to achieve via the relationship with the individual.

Important Differences for KLE Targets.

Just as there are some differences in approach for lethal versus nonlethal targets, there are some important requirements for KLE targeting that do not necessarily apply for other types of targets. This variation in application primarily occurs during the *decide* and *assessment* steps of the targeting process.

Decide. As previously discussed, targeting in COIN is about people, and KLE targeting is no exception. Conducting a KLE with a targeted individual is essentially the beginning of a relationship instead of a discrete event. That relationship can be used to achieve a variety of effects from which a commander can choose. As such, FSEC carefully crafted each KLE to achieve a broad array of objectives depending on the position, affiliation, and assessed level of influence of the individual in question. In addition to a specific objective for meeting with the engagement target, each KLE had at least three additional purposes: (1) to gain each individual's assessment of the current political, social, or security climate, (2) to deliver specific messages from coalition forces and/or FSEC relevant to national reconciliation, and (3) to evaluate the influence and reconciliation potential of each individual in ongoing and future reconciliation initiatives. KLE and the fact that it involves people also requires that commanders view each engagement not as an end in itself but, rather, in terms if its potential to achieve an end within one line of engagement. Specifically, commanders cannot look at a single engagement with a single effect as a possibility; they should view an engagement target as one with which a series of engagements might occur as the relationship develops. It would be unreasonable, for example, for FSEC to expect an important Iraqi shaykh to use his contacts to help with a reconciliation project during the first meeting or perhaps even the second.

Deciding how and when to conduct an engagement is akin to choosing the appropriate ammunition to target enemy forces in conventional warfare. However, it is arguably more difficult to discern how a meeting venue and timing will affect the outcome of an engagement than in evaluating how a lethal munition will affect its target. Commanders conducting KLE must also be able to understand the security, political, and reputational sensitivities of the engagement target as well as how to approach the individual before making that decision.

Finally, determining the sequencing of the engagements is somewhat more nuanced for KLE than conventional targets. Like conventional targeting, sequencing is important; it may be, for example, more beneficial to meet with one group of individuals before or after another depending on the objectives of the engagement and the character and nature of the groups being engaged. During FSEC's operations in Iraq, FSEC had to be careful not to offend an intended engagement target by meeting with his rival first (or allowing that meeting to become known). And, in some cases, FSEC had to obtain the permission of the Iraqi government before it could meet with some members of insurgent organizations and proceed with reconciliation initiatives.

Assess. In the conventional targeting process, the effects are almost always immediate. That is, it is comparatively easy to determine how effective the targeting was by the amount of damage the target sustained. In KLE targeting, however, the effects may not be so immediate, and measures of effectiveness are much more difficult to identify and ascertain. If a commander seeks a specific effect—such as brokering a meeting between a local shaykh and a representative of a provincial government—identifying whether or not that effect was achieved is relatively easy. If, however, a commander seeks a more general effect—such as a cessation of hostilities between two opposing groups or an engagement target keeping good on his word to convince an insurgent leader to talk to the Iraqi government representative, the effects are not so easily discernable. In those cases, intelligence becomes even more important, as well as the quality of the relationship between the unit and the engagement target.

There is one additional difference between conventional targeting and unconventional that KLE operations reveal; sometimes targets can shift from lethal to nonlethal and vice versa. The Anbar outreach is a case in point; shaykhs and other Iraqis who collaborated with al-Qaida were initially identified as hostile and were typically targeted lethally; once they decided not to work with al-Qaida anymore, they were approached with nonlethal means, including offers of employment and KLE.

FSEC AND INFORMATION OPERATIONS

KLE in any form is also a means commanders can use to deliver messages to the local population. In that sense, executing KLE operations can be part of an Information Operations (IO) strategy. The FSEC mission, as well as the messaging it developed and conducted as part of its KLE strategy, covered several principles of IO recommended by U.S. COIN doctrine.

FM 3-24 identifies IO in COIN as one of the most "decisive" of the various lines of operations used.[30] The IO section of the manual directs commanders to "consider encouraging host-nation leaders to provide a forum for initiating a dialogue with the opposition." Noting that this type of dialogue "does not equate to 'negotiating with terrorists,' the FM continues that the dialogue should "... attempt to open the door to mutual understanding. . . if counterinsurgents are talking with their adversaries, they are using a positive approach and may learn something useful. If the host nation is reluctant to communicate with insurgents, other counterinsurgents may have to initiate contact."[31]

The genesis of FSEC was a direct application of these guidelines. FSEC was established to "initiate contact" between Iraqi insurgent organizations and the Iraqi government. By directly engaging with the adversaries of MNF-I and the Iraqi government at the strategic level, FSEC attempted to bring disparate elements together, develop discreet communications channels that those elements could use, and, in so doing, facilitate Sunni and Shi'a-oriented national reconciliation initiatives.

IO proscriptions for COIN also acknowledge that the host-nation government is much more effective at transmitting messages to its population than the diplomatic or military representatives of an intervening force. FM 3-24 advises that commanders instead "encourage host-nation officials to handle" the delivery of information to constituents themselves.[32] Recognizing that effective counterinsurgents "work to convince insurgent leaders that the time for resistance is ended and that other ways to accomplish what they desire exist," similar guidelines would follow for portions of the population loyal to the insurgent leadership. Insurgent leaders have far more credibility when speaking to their followers than an outside force or international media would. FSEC messaging during engagements frequently provided the engagement targets with information about the Coalition stance on "acceptable" types of resistance,[33] that the Coalition was supportive of reconciliation between insurgent and government, and things of that nature. Those individuals, in turn, had the opportunity to transmit those messages in a manner that their constituents would find acceptable and translate those messages into appropriate actions.

Finally, IO guidelines charge counterinsurgents to "learn the insurgents' messages or narratives" and "develop counter-messages and counter-narratives to attack the insurgents' ideology."[34] One of the by-products of conducting engagements was that FSEC engagers frequently obtained information about rumors on the street and popular perceptions of various groups and individuals. FSEC engagers were, furthermore, frequently subjected to the ideological narratives of insurgent groups, the Iraqi government, and the Iraqi people caught in between. Over time, FSEC developed responses to many of the Iraqis' complaints and requests for clarification, sometimes with assistance from the MNF-I Strategic Communications directorate, but often based on guidance from policymakers and the MNF-I commander. Unfortunately, KLE was not often incorporated into IO-related targeting or strategies across theater.

INTELLIGENCE IN COIN AND FSEC INTELLIGENCE REQUIREMENTS

Intelligence is a critical element of the targeting process; without good intelligence, effective targeting cannot occur. KLE targeting is no exception, but the focus for intelligence targeting for those types of targets—people—is different. Recalling that veto players are the individuals most likely to be able to achieve the desired effects with an insurgent group or other segment of a population, the intelligence support to the targeting process in KLE targeting should be on those people.

FSEC's Information Requirements and Sources of Intelligence.

FSEC's KLE targeting focused on identifying both potential reconciliation initiatives and veto players who could contribute to national reconciliation. Although the FSEC mission had numerous information requirements, it focused on four categories of information in particular:

- Information that could cue FSEC about ongoing reconciliation initiatives and key personnel who could be used as interlocutors to link FSEC into the reconciliation process.
- Information about the status of these reconciliation efforts, how the people and parties affected by the initiatives were impacted, and some sense of what the people involved believed the role for FSEC/Coalition forces should have been.
- Information that would allow FSEC and the Coalition to identify which individuals and organizations in the insurgent/armed group population were potentially reconcilable, and those who were irreconcilable.
- FSEC sought to maximize the reconciliation value of those identified as reconcilable by assessing the individual or group's *level of influence*; that is, the ability of those individuals to influence others to cease their unhelpful activities and peacefully transition to the political process.[35]

FSEC used several sources of information to meet these requirements. In addition to information and atmospherics garnered from FSEC engagements, FSEC relied upon five main sources of information to satisfy its requirements: Open-source (unclassified) reporting (OSINT), Human Intelligence (HUMINT) reporting from both national and tactical collection entities, Signals Intelligence (SIGINT), diplomatic reporting, and feedback from other MNF-I elements' KLE. Of those sources, some of the best for the FSEC mission came from OSINT, diplomatic reporting, and detainees held in Coalition custody.

Some of the more critical FSEC information needs were met by the use of OSINT. FSEC had access to daily media digests and OSINT summaries produced by the MNF-I OSINT cell and the Media Operations Center (MOC). In addition, a substantial amount of academic literature was available on Iraq, its regions, and ethno-religious communities within Iraq from nongovernmental organizations (NGOs) and regional specialists who helped FSEC better understand the background and contacts of the ongoing political and military disputes in the country. Translation of some documents obtained in the course of engagements also yielded some important information about the Iraqi government's strategy and intentions. Other sources of OSINT key to the FSEC mission included polling data on Iraq's political parties; International Crisis Group (ICG) products; and Iraq country studies produced by the Rand Corporation, Strategic Studies Institute, and other think-tanks.

Diplomatic reporting, too, was an excellent fit for FSEC's needs. Records of diplomatic engagements often provided unique perspectives on personalities and political entities within the context of politics, political atmospherics, and Iraqi government existing and intended policies. In theaters like Iraq, the value of diplomatic reporting was enhanced with Provincial Reconstruction Team (PRT) reporting, which frequently provided FSEC with Iraqi street-level perspectives on a variety of situations and incidents. At the tactical level, the Coalition military units that had reconciliation or civil affairs cells responsible for conducting KLE in support of reconciliation occasionally provided feedback on their engagements, which was also useful to the FSEC mission.

The reconciliation value of the detainee population was perhaps most surprising. Most MNF-I entities viewed the detainees as a source of intelligence support to lethal—versus non-lethal—operations. While FM 3-24 identifies detainees as a good source of intelligence because of the "information they provide about the internal workings of insurgency," it makes no reference to the reconciliation value of the detainees.[36] Many of the individuals in Coalition custody were leaders of, or had significant influence within, various insurgent groups operating in Iraq. Some of those detainees had valuable insights about which elements of those groups were reconcilable and how the Iraqi government could best reach out to those groups to encourage a departure from violence. In addition, a few detainees had the ability to influence insurgent groups to transition to the political process *while still in detention.* However, there was little acknowledgement or understanding of how to use detainees for reconciliation purposes and, thus, little effort to direct collection efforts of that nature at the detainee population.

Problems Fulfilling Information Requirements.

Identifying FSEC's information and intelligence requirements was difficult at first and was ultimately achieved via trial and error. Fulfilling those requirements had its own set of challenges. In general, intelligence collection agencies at the operational and strategic level in Iraq tended to be more focused on political party and political entity reporting, as well as lethal targeting-related reporting; little emphasis was placed on the reconciliation opportunities and individuals associated with them. In addition, some collection agencies did not appear interested in collecting information about an individual or group's reconciliation value or level of influence within a given community. As a result, there was also a dearth of finished, fused product reporting on reconciliation initiatives and key personalities involved in reconciliation efforts. Although FSEC obtained some fused products from the Multi-National Corps-Iraq (MNC-I) analysis cell and some national-level intelligence products on key personalities, FSEC spent a great deal of time fusing reconciliation-related products (bios of engagement targets, assessments of initiatives, briefings, etc.)—a tremendous workload for what was a very small group of analysts and engagers.

ADDITIONAL CHALLENGES, RECOMMENDATIONS, AND RISKS

In addition to the challenges already discussed, FSEC had a number of other difficulties to overcome in the conduct of its operations. Many of the difficulties also apply more broadly to KLE missions. Those challenges were of two types: (1) the technical difficulties associated with conducting and integrating FSEC KLE operations with others in theater, and (2) cultural issues that minimized the effectiveness of FSEC KLE operations.

Technical Challenges.

Synchronization of effort. FSEC had difficulty with synchronizing its engagements with other KLE missions in theater as well as missions conducive to reconciliation initiatives. At the operational and tactical level, most Coalition military units were already conducting KLE to generate peace and stability in their areas of operation. At the strategic level, Coalition diplomats conducted their own engagements to achieve policy objectives with key Iraqi government personnel, build the capacity of Iraqi ministries, and effect national reconciliation via political organizations. In addition to FSEC—which was established later than some other MNF-I directorates—the Force Strategic Effects directorate was devoted to strategic engagements designed to build Iraqi government capacity, conduct outreach to religious entities, conduct information operations, and infrastructure reconstruction. Although the leaders of these entities routinely met with each other to synchronize their efforts and different cells contacted each other on an ad-hoc basis, no formalized mechanism organized and synchronized each organization's engagements across theater. Since many of the desired effects from those engagements were potentially mutually supportive, the lack of synchronization resulted in a combination of overlap and underachievement on some important issues. FSEC often found itself stumbling on diplomats' established territory with respect to engaging Iraqi government officials and political party leaders and was not always synchronized with Force Information Operations objectives. At the same time, FSEC frequently needed to link reconciliation initiatives with hard deliverables—such as improved infrastructure, vocational-technical programs to reintegrate former insurgents, etc.—that were being implemented by the Strategic Effects directorate. And, although FSEC repeatedly attempted to incorporate other agencies, directorates, and Coalition units into its targeting process to avoid these pitfalls, many agencies and directorates chose not to participate.

Recommendation: Establish a theater-level targeting board to synchronize KLE and related efforts at the strategic level, or incorporate all nonlethal effects, including KLE, into an existing theater joint-targeting board.

The lack of a synchronized engagement strategy also resulted in reporting problems. Much of the KLE ongoing at the tactical and operational level had strategic implications (and vice versa), but most units did not keep records of the KLE conducted by unit commanders, soldiers, etc., within their area of operations. By the same token, units conducting operations at those levels had difficulty gaining situational awareness of the reconciliation initiatives and other KLE ongoing at the strategic level that affected their areas of responsibility because they had no means of access to the reporting at that level. And, despite FSEC's efforts to post the executive summaries of its engagements in a variety of locations accessible to Coalition units, most units had not been incorporating KLE into their targeting boards or other operations; therefore, they saw little need to access KLE reporting from FSEC or any other units.

Recommendation: Institutionalize KLE as an essential part of targeting and operations in COIN and incorporate KLE reporting into intelligence reporting and intelligence databases available to units operating in theater.

Continuity. In *Defeating Communist Insurgency*, Sir Robert Thompson identified that the British success in the Malayan Emergency was, in part, a result of continuity with key personnel who worked with the insurgents and/or the established Malayan government.[37] Iraq and other theaters involving insurgencies are no exception. One of the keys to successful engagement outcomes was FSEC's ability to develop and sustain relationships with important Iraqi government personnel, tribal shaykhs, and insurgent group representatives. The FSEC rotation cycle, however, was not conducive to the continuity of those relationships. While the FSEC director and Ambassador's representative worked in FSEC for 12-month tours, most of the FSEC officers were only in country for 6 months (with some exceptions). At the time a relationship between FSEC and a KLE target was just beginning to solidify, FSEC would experience a changeover in personnel; new personnel would then have to spend time rebuilding rapport with the Iraqis, who were constantly being introduced to new faces amid the development of some sensitive issues. In some cases, the FSEC replacement was simply unable to reenergize the relationship after a trusted FSEC officer's departure. Some of the Iraqis complained that they never knew which FSEC representative they would be meeting, and at least a few were reluctant to continue the relationship without the presence of the trusted FSEC officer.

The other problem with high turnover related to the volume of information new arrivals had to consume. Effective engagements necessitated a working knowledge of the key issues between the Iraqi government and insurgent group and an understanding of the history behind how those relations deteriorated and/or became reinvigorated. Most FSEC engagers arrived in theater with little understanding of the situation, and acquiring that knowledge base took 3-4 months, depending on the individual. By the time many of the engagers had that knowledge, they were only 2 months away from leaving the country.

Recommendation. Engagement cell personnel should be assigned for a period of at least 2 years, with regularly scheduled leave periods. Transition time between incoming and outgoing engagers should be at least 2 months.

Capability. Most military personnel are not diplomats, and few have exposure to diplomatic operations or training.[38] FSEC officers were no exception. Most of the FSEC personnel in the organization from 2008-09 had no formal training or experiences in diplomacy, negotiation, or KLE more broadly and, for some, it was a somewhat awkward transition to an engagement role. FSEC's one career diplomat—the representative of the U.S. Ambassador—did show, through his example, some diplomatic techniques. In addition, FSEC was equipped with an excellent cultural advisor of Middle Eastern descent who was always prepared to assist the FSEC engagers with Iraqi cultural norms, practices, and expectations. For most of FSEC, however, it was a case of learning by doing. Some officers struggled and others excelled; success depended largely on the officer and his or her initiative in learning a productive approach or using the interpersonal skills he/she acquired during his/her time in service. In cases where the officer struggled, the relationship with the Iraqi engagement targets suffered, which was detrimental to the overall mission.

Recommendation: Provide training or, at a minimum, exposure to the conduct of diplomatic operations to personnel in units that will be responsible for conducting KLE beyond the occasional encounter during predeployment training. If KLE cells were to be incorporated into other U.S. COIN operations, it would be important to focus on training and development for personnel best suited to those engagements. Foreign Area Officers (FAOs) have a niche here; unfortunately, the U.S. Army and Marine Corps FAO programs lack the requisite number of FAOs to meet the mission requirements. Given that only a limited number of those conducting KLE will have regional expertise, a long "right-seat ride" between outgoing and incoming personnel is essential for success.

Cultural Challenges.

The dimension of time and expectations. Militaries are trained to be effects-oriented, and often the expectation is that those effects will be immediate. These expectations tend to result in impatience with establishing and building the relationships necessary to brokering useful dialogue. All too often, commanders expect that the desired outcome of a relationship or KLE can be achieved in a single engagement or very few engagements, and that direct engagement with an insurgent group leader, important members of the government, etc., is the best approach since it is the most direct approach. During FSEC's operations, the failure to exercise patience with the development of relationships and to recognize that an indirect approach to an engagement target could be beneficial put some important relationships at risk or stalled them altogether.

In many cultures, and the Iraqi culture in particular, it is important to develop a relationship before asking someone to reciprocate. While Westerners tend to see relationships as tit-for-tat, Iraqi culture does not function in that manner. Multi-National Division Baghdad Reconciliation Cell leader Colonel Richard Welch mentioned that Iraqis consider it rude to be asked for anything or to do anything before a relationship has been properly established.[39] FSEC cultural advisor Ihab Ali often advised that the objective of the initial engagements with Iraqis should be to establish trust through sincerity and respect—two very important factors in Arab culture stemming from different societal conditions in the Middle East. Those conditions—particularly fear of exploitation—tend to make Arabs very suspicious of outsiders. Therefore, one might have to take several steps with the Iraqis before they could be reasonably expected to reciprocate. Once the Iraqi was convinced that the relationship was worth pursuing, however, the Iraqi would stop at nothing to assist FSEC or other personnel who engaged them.[40]

In addition, Iraqi leaders typically send representatives or interlocutors to negotiate on their behalf; rarely does a principal Iraqi decisionmaker engage directly with Coalition/other Iraqi leaders. If Iraqi principals did meet with FSEC, they tended to speak broadly and make vague commitments or none at all. The coalition tendency to sometimes ignore the value of interlocutors in an endeavor to go straight to the principal resulted in missed opportunities and misunderstandings on some important issues.

Interagency difficulties. FSEC's difficulties working with other agencies were similar to those experienced by other military and intelligence organizations thrust together in Iraq. FSEC did, however, face some additional skepticism from some of the intelligence agencies and career diplomats in the U.S. Department of State working in Baghdad. Many of the diplomats supported the FSEC mission and, in cases where the mission overlapped, the diplomats worked closely with FSEC personnel to initiate and support reconciliation initiatives. Others dismissed FSEC as a military organization in its entirely and refused to coordinate engagements with FSEC.

Although FSEC did not have the diplomatic experience or knowledge of the career diplomats, the military processes FSEC used to organize its engagements—the U.S. military targeting process in particular—served as an excellent model for engagements more broadly. The targeting process coupled with FSEC's procedure for writing and reporting engagements was, arguably, more organized, more focused, and more accessible and digestible than the processes and reporting procedures used by some other agencies.

Recommendation: The U.S. diplomatic corps should consider institutionalizing the U.S. military targeting process or similar mechanism to structure its engagements in embassies abroad, with emphasis on those theaters containing a significant U.S. military presence.

Additional Risks Associated with the FSEC Mission and KLE.

While FSEC's outreach to insurgents via KLE yielded some benefits, KLE of that nature was not without risk. Specifically, the Coalition risked supporting an Iraqi government cell and program that lacked longevity and/or legitimacy, and the insurgent groups that FSEC engaged could have used the engagements and related meetings as stalling techniques; targeting of specific individuals or groups was suspended for engagement purposes from time to time.

We have already discussed the importance of host-nation government legitimacy during COIN operations. After the 2005 elections, the Iraqi government struggled to establish its legitimacy; it was widely viewed as corrupt and, as the violence escalated, was incapable of securing its citizens on its own. The Iraqi government was, furthermore, perceived to be a "puppet" of an occupying force and acting in its own interests rather than that of the Iraqi people. Since insurgent groups and citizens alike viewed the Iraqi government as illegitimate for a variety of reasons, linking reconciliation initiatives with the government was also viewed with suspicion.

The legitimacy problem also illustrates why setting up a reconciliation-related strategic engagement cell in Afghanistan would be difficult, if not impossible. The Afghan government is widely viewed as corrupt and ineffective by the Afghan population.[41] There is no legitimate government entity with which Coalition forces could engage in Afghanistan, and engaging with insurgent organizations without tying them to the Afghan government risks the development of solutions only sustainable as long as the Coalition remains in Afghanistan.

FSEC took some more unambiguous risks with the insurgents groups it engaged with. When FSEC conducted engagements with individuals affiliated with those insurgent groups, those individuals were placed on a Restricted Target List or RTL that precluded other Coalition elements from capturing them. Under some circumstances, targeting of a whole organization could be suspended as well. It was possible—if not probable—that the insurgent groups would use that "grace period" as an opportunity to stall for time and organize operations against the Coalition and/or the Iraqi government without the fear that Coalition or Iraqi forces would detain members of the group. The insurgent groups could also use the period to flee the country. In most cases, however, those groups that were interested in dealing with FSEC and/or the Iraqi government already believed themselves to be cornered or were seeking alternative means of pursuing their objectives.

CONCLUSION

Whether or not cells like FSEC or a Division G-7 are designated to conduct KLE in support of reconciliation, leaders in units conducting COIN operations will, at some point, have to conduct KLE in some form. The U.S. military has had commanders doing just that since the onset of post-invasion operations in Iraq. However, FSEC operations strongly indicate that an organized effort focused on KLE and synchronization of KLE using the targeting process can better maximize the utility and value of such engagements with the understanding that those efforts must be tied to the efforts of a legitimate host-nation government. An established process for conducting and reporting on KLE also forces diplomats, military commanders, and others involved in the process to develop and operate within a clear strategy rather than via haphazard engagements that may or may not be linked to ongoing efforts in information operations, intelligence, and things of that nature. That strategy could ultimately be integrated with a unit's other COIN efforts and has the potential to complement those efforts at comparatively little cost in terms of resources.

Some principles of practices in other insurgencies and FSEC operations in Iraq also demonstrate that there is some value in outreach to insurgent organizations, even if they have targeted host-nation and outside forces in the past. Although there are some risks associated with that particular brand of KLE, the benefits can far outweigh the costs; commanders can expend energies on building local relationships and then use those relationships to stabilize an area rather than attempting to seek out and destroy every single insurgent in the sector. Furthermore, almost all operations entail a certain amount of risk; it is up to the commanders or leaders to find the means of mitigating that risk. As long as the efforts of this type of KLE remain tied to the reconciliation efforts of a legitimate host-nation government or government representative, the risks are kept to a minimum.

FSEC operations provide only one example of how units operating in Iraq used KLE to initiate and further reconciliation. Anecdotes from several personnel involved with reconciliation in the Multi-National Divisions (MND-Ds) from 2007-09 indicate that some units developed their own strategy to broker dialogue with members of organizations involved in destructive activities in their battle spaces. Although this article does not attempt to "prove" that this type of KLE is effective, perhaps one anecdote about what can happen when a unit does not use this type of technique in COIN best illustrates the necessity for KLE strategies. Colonel Richard Welch had the opportunity to observe how four different divisions in Baghdad conducted operations and observed that:

> Unfortunately, when [the incoming unit] rolled into town to replace [the outgoing unit], the [new unit] shut down every major engagement plan and program we had because they said, "we aren't here to make friends, we are here to finish the job we started in 2003 during the invasion (i.e., combat operations)." I was here for 6 months following the [outgoing unit's] departure, and it was ugly what [the incoming unit] did. In my personal and professional opinion, it is one of the main reasons we lost the city to massive sectarian violence in 2005-2006—because [units in Baghdad] had lost visibility of what was going on in the city due to the lack of a coordinated engagement strategy.[42]

Effective KLE is, furthermore, only one persuasive technique available to commanders engaging in COIN operations; however, it can be a tremendous force multiplier if employed effectively and may be essential to success in today's COIN environments in Iraq and perhaps Afghanistan as well.

Insurgencies in already divided societies create enormously intricate dynamics, and, though an intervening force may be of assistance or even a requirement to return the situation to normalcy, the presence of an outside COIN often serves to compound that situation's complexity. In addition, each civil war involving an insurgency is unique, and the requirements of an intervening force are likely to be determined more by the setting in which it finds itself rather than a "cookie cutter" series of solutions. FSEC and its mission were one mechanism that was useful in the Iraq scenario, and some of its basic operations have applications to the conduct of U.S. COIN operations more generally. How those concepts are implemented rests with the environment in which they are employed and the commanders that must operate within them.

ENDNOTES

1. Carlotta Gall, "Insurgents in Afghanistan are Gaining, Petraeus Says," *New York Times,* October 1, 2008.

2. Colonel Richard Welch, Interview, November 2008. Colonel Welch was the Multi-National Division Baghdad Reconciliation Cell Director from 2006-09. He served in Baghdad from 2004-05 and from 2006 until the present in a civil affairs and reconciliation capacity. He was responsible for Key Leader Engagements in the Baghdad area of responsibility and observed first hand how the presence or absence of an engagement strategy impacted the Baghdad area. I had an opportunity to witness something similar in Northern Iraq in 2003-04 in comparing the operations of the 101st Airborne Division (Air Assault) in Mosul, Iraq, and the 4th Infantry Division in Tikrit. While the 101st had an engagement strategy of sorts, the 4th ID was more focused on kinetic operations; the 101st area remained more peaceful and stable than the 4th ID area, in general.

3. Major Niel Smith and Colonel Sean MacFarland, U.S. Army, "Anbar Awakens: The Tipping Point," *Military Review*, March-April 2008, pp. 41-52.

4. Sources and authorities on conflict resolution and my own experiences in Iraq and Bosnia view reconciliation as a phased process, where reconciliation is defined as "restoring relationships and learning to live nonviolently with radical differences." Oliver Ramsbotham, Tom Woodhouse, and Hugh Miall, *Contemporary Conflict Resolution: The Prevention, Management, and Transformations of Deadly Conflict*, Cambridge, United Kingdom: Polity Press, 1999, pp. 231. The initial phases of reconciliation tend to involve opening communications channels between the various parties,

ceasefires, confidence-building measures, and things of that nature. Reconciliation occurs after these phases, and often takes years. Reconciliation, too, is almost always a function of the host-nation government finding a means to incorporate or accommodate insurgent organizations politically, which is discussed later in this paper.

5. David M. Tressler, *Negotiation in the New Strategic Environment: Lessons from Iraq*, Carlisle, PA: Strategic Studies Institute: U.S. Army War College, August 2007.

6. FM 3-24 is a compilation of several other manuals that outline U.S. military doctrine, including Information Operations and Targeting Doctrine. I chose to use FM 3-24 as the primary reference because it synthesizes much existing Army doctrine, not because I believe it is necessarily an improvement upon that doctrine.

7. David Galulah, *Counterinsurgency Warfare: Theory and Practice,* Westport, CT: Praeger Security International, 2006, pp. 3-10. There is a similar description in Bard O'Neill's *Insurgency and Terrorism: From Revolution to Apocalypse*, Washington, DC: Brassey's (US), Inc., 2001.

8. U.S. Army and Marine Corps, *Counterinsurgency Field Manual*, Chicago, IL: University of Chicago Press, 2007, p. 105.

9. Ian Beckett, *Modern Insurgencies and Counterinsurgencies: Guerillas and their Opponents since 1750*, New York: Routledge, 2005. Beckett identified a substantial increase in the use of "hearts and minds" strategies by counterinsurgents in the latter half of the 20th century, including British, American, French, and some other forces.

10. Ian Beckett, *Encyclopedia of Guerilla Warfare*, Santa Barbara, CA: ABC-CLIO Inc., 1999, p. 98. Although "hearts and minds" has been used to describe a variety of strategies that involve primarily persuasive measures applied against an adversary, the original description of the strategy by Sir Gerald Templar in the Malayan conflict is much more specific.

11. Stathis Kalyvas, *The Logic of Violence in Civil War*, New York: Cambridge University Press, 2006, Chap. 2.

12. David Elliot, *The Vietnamese War: Revolution and Social Change in the Mekong Delta 1930-1975*, Vol. II, Chap. 17, Armonk, NY: M. E. Sharp Inc., 2002.

13. Cliff Staten, "From Terrorism to Legitimacy: Political Opportunity Structures and the Case of Hezbollah," *The Online Journal of Peace and Conflict Resolution*, Vol. 8, No. 1, 2008, pp. 32-49, especially p. 38.

14. Barbara F. Walter, "Designing Transitions from Civil War," Barbara F. Walter and Jack Snyder, eds., *Civil Wars, Insecurity, and Intervention*, New York: Columbia University Press, 1999.

15. Staten, pp. 32-49.

16. Max Manwaring and John Fishel, "Insurgency and Counterinsurgency: Towards a New Analytical Approach," in *Small Wars and Insurgencies*, Vol. 3, No. 3, Winter 1992, p. 274. Manwaring and Fishel conducted their own empirical analysis of different insurgency models and concluded that legitimacy is vital to maintaining popular support and thus winning a civil war.

17. Staten, pp. 32-49.

18. Oliver Ramsbotham, Tom Woodhouse, and Hugh Miall, *Contemporary Conflict Resolution*, 2nd Ed., Boston, MA: Polity Press, 2005, p. 166.

19. George Tsebelis, "Decision Making in Political Systems: Veto Players in Presidentialism, Parliamentarism, Multicameralism, and Multipartyism," *British Journal of Political Science*, Vol. 24, No. 3, July 1995, pp. 289-325.

20. Ned Parker, "Iraq's Awakening: Two Tales Illustrate Force's Birth and Slow Death," *Los Angeles Times*, April 28, 2009, *www.latimes.com/news/nationworld/world/la-fg-iraq-awakening28-2009apr28,0,115151.story*.

21. Smith and MacFarland, pp. 41-43; Welch, interview.

22. "Britain's Armed Forces: Losing Their Way?" *The Economist,* January 31-February 6, 2009, pp. 61-62.

23. Carlotta Gall, "Insurgents in Afghanistan are Gaining, Petraeus Says," in *New York Times,* October 1, 2008, *www.nytimes. com/2008/10/01/world/asia/01petraeus.html.*

24. FM 3-24, p. 191.

25. *Ibid.,* pp. 192-193. (Emphasis by author.)

26. *Ibid.,* p. 193.

27. I am indebted to one of my Military Intelligence Captain's Career Course instructors (who wished to remain anonymous) for pointing out this fact in earlier drafts of the paper. I had originally viewed FSEC's use of the targeting process as a modification of existing doctrine when, in fact, the processes are identical.

28. Lieutenant Colonel Isaiah Wilson III, "Thinking Beyond War: Civil-Military Operational Planning in Northern Iraq," paper delivered at the Peace Studies Program, Cornell University, October 14, 2004.

29. The Reconciliation Annex to MNF-I's Joint Campaign Plan of 2007-08 is and remains classified; therefore, the specific goals could not be used in this paper.

30. FM 3-24, p. 160.

31. *Ibid.,* p. 162.

32. *Ibid.* Commanders are encouraged not to "attempt to explain actions by the host-nation government."

33. There are many forms of resistance, only one of which is violence. Acceptable forms of resistance in Iraq included peaceful demonstrations, written work, protest votes, and things of that nature.

34. FM 3-24, p. 162.

35. The level of influence could also be termed an individual's *social capital* or type of *authority* vested in an individual, see FM 3-24, p. 96-97. However, neither term is descriptive enough to explain the concept of influence, which has more power as a stand-alone term.

36. *Ibid.*, p. 121.

37. Sir Robert Thompson, *Defeating Communist Insurgency*, New York: F. A. Praeger, 1966, Chap. 2.

38. David Tressler, *Negotiations in the New Strategic Environment: Lessons from Iraq*, Carlisle, PA: Strategic Studies Institute, U.S. Army War College, 2007. Tressler notes that the U.S. military training centers are attempting to incorporate negotiation techniques into their training at various levels of command; however, not all KLEs will require negotiation, and preparation for KLE itself likely remains very basic.

39. Welch, interview.

40. Mr. Ihab Ali, Interview, September 2008. Mr. Ihab Ali was the cultural advisor to FSEC from its inception until October 2008.

41. J. Alexander Thier, *The Future of Afghanistan*, Washington, DC: United States Institute for Peace, 2009, pp. 1-13.

42. Welch, interview.